COYOTE SUN

To Joyce & Jay

Thanks

CARLOS CUMPIÁN

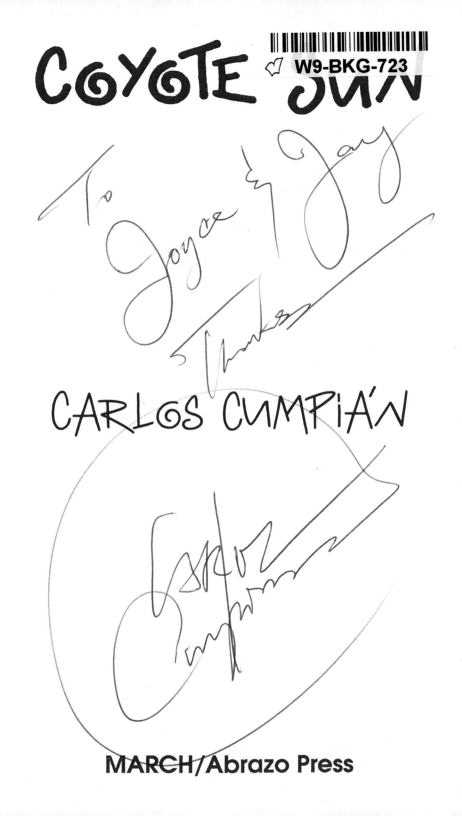

MARCH/Abrazo Press

Acknowledgments

These poems have appeared in the following
publications: *Exquisite Corpse: A Monthly*,
"New 'Official' Exquisite Corpse Psalm," 1988;
Rocky Mountain Arsenal of the Arts, "Cups,"
"Sunday, February 1988," 1986-89; *Salome:
A Literary Dance Magazine*, "Shiva" (Pinup),
1985; *Fiesta in Aztlan Anthology*, "Cuento"
(reprint), 1982; *Tonatzin*, "America Needs
'Operation Jobs'", 1985; *Notebook: A Little Maga-
zine* (Raza Cosmica issue), "Veterano," 1987; *Nit
& Wit*, "¿Pork Que No?" 1979; *Spoon River Quar-
terly*, "The New Job," 1979; *American Indian
News*, "The Survivor: Anishinabe Man" (reprint),
1983; *RAM Raza Arts Media*, "After Wrestling
Away Rain Forests," 1977; *Left Curve Magazine*,
"Property is Theft," 1978; *ECOS*, "Kilotons and
Then Some," 1985; *Literati Chicago*, "Muralist
Incantation," 1988; *Emergency Tacos Anthology*,
"Coyote Rides the Bus," 1989.

Art by Carlos A. Cortez
Photo by Kim Johnson

For further information or copies, write to:
MARCH/Abrazo Press
PO Box 2890
Chicago, Illinois 60690

For my elders

Jesusa
Antonio
María
Miguel
Juanita
Ramiro
Mariana
Carlos

Table of Contents

Table of Contents

"Who Do You Love?"

"I walk 47 miles of barbed wire
use a cobra snake for a necktie
I got a brand-new house on the roadside
made from rattlesnake hide
...now come on take a little walk
with me honey and tell me,
who do you love?"

—Bo Diddley

The "Official" Exquisite Corpse Psalm

(based on the 23rd psalm)
for Andrei Codrescu

The Lord is my editor,
I shall not wander in streams of consciousness,
He checks my grammar, syntax, and ellipsis,
He proofs and types to put me at ease,
He reissues good copy,
out of print books
and articles.
He is my sole distributor.

Above Drudgery

for Cynthia

to be Aphrodite today
must be confusing
no one knows a real goddess
when they see one—
no one has the paunch
of patient concern anymore—
flat bellies or nothing.
O archangel of desire
i keep my shirt on while
your apricot mouth
castigates a whole
generation.
your conch shell ears
offer evidence amid
the grimace of
ordinary faces,
your old boyfriend cyclops
reads the paper,
his sunglasses the
size of cymbals.
your damp deity body
lays on a used towel,
while my eyes dehydrate
from following you
like a gladiator
in the desert.

Cups

Turned up,
posted to dry on
ivory wire rack,
turquoise baked round
in a sheen of
tranquility next to the
bright white one,
where yellow fields of
fat doves are poised
to scatter before the
morning's black tonic
of hot café hits
each rim,
two cups with
unchipped handles,
touching
without
lips.

My Gifted Friend

Amaranth and serpentine madras
mix with orange blossoms to seal
their tint into water and fabric.
A sleepy yellow offers the pale
moon its pollen light and silence.
You did not know the violet flame
an artist steals
is a kiss that lasts for weeks,
then one day it merges with green,
promising a healing.
Lingering fingers of white,
refractured in the snow line
as late summer blazes,
pretty girls become women.
From a palette of
hazel-brown eyes some
serenade and study
those shoulder-length swirls
and perfect spirals I get lost in,
until nearing your emerald lobes,
where firm hands balance the
portrait of your breath
before the big fiesta.

After Calling

Sola mi
abuela
has my ear
at home
under a San Antonio
año nuevo
moon

In Chicago I hear
her complaints
and promise
the pain will go away
before we need to
hang up
alone.

Sunday, February 1988

It wasn't from TV Guide we read,
going round-robin, four voices
out of three books—
Calvino docked in maritime ports
where every love is a salutation.
Dorn grew roots from
pastoral melodies, giving
minerals and animals full consideration.
Koch, the word coach, crazy editor
to budding urban bards, savoring
simple lies, wishes, and dreams.
Little "Who-lee" pointed and repeated
letters off the dark green cover,
as we each took turns in our
evening winter circle.

Muralist Incantation

Summer ricans gathered into
former littered lot,
where waves of concerns are
burned away, no more trash
to see, no bent splintered
floors, rotting doors to
feel a whole lot better with
our youth in view.
Hanging out the banner of
our smiles made of warmth,
aqui, on these once
glass-smashed sidewalks,
we worked hard
con multi-colored hands,
dabbin' strokin' half-naked
we take out
our passions for slappin'
la conga and get you into
this minor masterpiece,
'cause we want the magic
of our African/Spanish/Taino
destinos to mix
mambo y salsa realities,
we can dance today
under our island and mainland
star before the weather
does a broken-treaty number
on us all, and change what
strength we painted
on this wall—
charged with the juice of
neon-soaked streets.

Pinup

She stayed all day beneath
dark green shades
sucking tall
Italian
lemonades.
Layed in shadows
away from coastal
Mayan heat
melting pounds
of crystallized
sweets.

Burning styrofoam makes
chloroflurocarbons,
modern eraser of the air.
Piled up cup
after cup
at her beach bar,
she worries if maybe
she's been extravagant.

Ultraviolet lights,
heat lumps of
copal-amber incense
releasing sweet smoke
with its greasy flame.
Slipping
black cloves -- cool
onto her tongue
licks shut her
hand-rolled
"good night cigarette."

Apart from the Arsenal

Ya ya yawn y swallow
blink back the beer
behind your eyelids.
In the corner red flowers
have lost their muscles,
grow fat and pale without
sol-light, sun-luz,
in the room,
far from the border
where penguins take
their beaches serious.

Across the water
of our skinny river
neighbors sit on their
ledges to catch us without
nothing thicker than a
rubber between us.
We forget to pull the
curtains after looking
into each others' eyes.

The contour of our rings
were presented on pillows
still warm from swimming,
I remember nearly drowning,
spent too much time in
front of the tv & never learned
how to float. Ah, childhood,
so full of lies.

Now we are adults.
Faster and faster
we all go, getting
far enough from you
to miss your farts.
The yards of green
will balloon into
golden browns then
slowly fill with
white, before peeling
back to green again.

Another summer, flood hits
Greek and Mexican
garden apartments.
Airplanes filled with
Puerto Ricans may never
leave the runway, baggage
stuck on the old tarmac,
but they still feel at home.

Nobody not even
polar bears
with Korean
neighbors
will be alarmed
when the entire
city thaws.

Communion Waif-ers

From my apartment window
you can see dozens of trees
growing thick near the river's
edge.
Last night, just above the
tree line, I think I saw a
flying saucer.
Guess it were 'bout the size of
a Texas watermelon, only with the
seeds spat out.

Watermelons are not good places
for space travelers to hide.
Too many rattlers under 'em and
poor folks steal melons
right from the fields.
A blond bouffant on the head of
some chain-smoking bowler
would offer better
shelter.

You see, the aliens aren't
really very big and strong.
They need to be packed in cotton,
swaddled like a baby, sleep with an
air conditioner on
while soaking in alcohol.
They have to be allowed
to rest undisturbed
from their 500-year
invasion.

Universal Boor-Zhwäze Pleasure

Did you ever lean in and
press your thighs against
a cool ceramic urinal?
Not one of those upside
down helmets, posted half-
way up the wall,
rather, a full arched,
floor to chest high
amber-catching wonder.
There, you can let go
a fast head of stream,
allowing bladder busting
release through your
urethra,
of all that once useful
water—
that gives you life and
...ahhhh.

Barflies Have Feelings Too

I once dreamt about
old Charles
"poetry is like a good shit"
Bukowski.
He wanted a new look,
he was tired of
his mean reflection,
always getting lost in the
moon pores and liver lines.

Don't ask why he called me
at some loop bar,
a place even he wouldn't visit
to take a piss in.
So while swigging
a cold beer from Wisconsin
and reading the collection
of business cards
visible in the joint's fish bowl,
the phone rings, it's Bukowski,
wants me to find the names of
all the plastic surgeons...
up comes a card that reads:
"Discreet work from head to feet.
World's Best in all of South America.
VISA and MasterCard accepted."

Only the doctor had a long
German name and a p.o. box
in Buenos Aires, Argentina.
Bukowski said,

"Great, see you when I get back."
Before I could say, "Adios",
he's standing in front of me
showing off the results of his
trip to the doc,
his nose bark peeled and
pores filled with smooth pellets
of steel and wax.
It was a most manageable beak,
the nose he wanted at thirty,
he seemed satisfied, only wondered
if it was safe to pick.
To celebrate he pulled from a sack
a bottle of Irish whiskey,
raised a drink to his lips and sipped,
but when he put the booze down,
his old nose was back.

There's No Face at Home

I wasn't always big 'n ugly,
four-days growth of gray-grease stubble,
110 pounds of excess baggage,
seat belts barely fit,
what's left of my agility is
spent on the toilet.
I was once a carpenter, but I did
a royal number on some friend
of Ann Landers—
she wrote me up in that column of hers,
and reinforced everything
anybody had ever gossiped about me.

Since then, I haven't worked for weeks.
I'll stay calm as long as I can,
remembering what my friend Alfredo says,
"You can't get hurt
falling out of a basement window."
Soon I'll be evicted
and have to start over,
just as I was getting
used to this place.
Sure it's no mansion,
but it's no inch-thin noise
and roach receiver,
hell, at least I have smoke alarms.

I drive a faded red car
with mileage turned back to zero.
After ten years of commuting,
nothing on the radio
interests me,
so I play Bible tapes
bought at Kresskeys.

Advice

para Carlos Cortez Koyokuikatl

Tos, mi tocayo,
toma la operación,
so los doctores don't
think you as stubborn
as some matador's target.

If they cut you,
it's because they
got to...draw out
the unwanted
visitor in
your lung.

Since you
"launched your artistic career,"
back there with crayons
on the wall,
there's been no
stopping you...

linocuts, woodcuts,
indoor and outdoor
raw-raza murals,
fine-line figures on
scratchboards,
and paint mixed with
gouged furrows that
rise on once-smooth
surfaces willing to
bloom under your
two steady hands.

After all the posters you
made and exchanged,
collections rolled up
ready to unpack where
there's still barrios,
escuelas y
walls
waiting for your exhibit.

Si, ese take
el pinche
doctor's
advice,
even if you
get under the
bato's knife,
no more pirámides
made of cigarrillo
ash, those all day smokes
and collection
of Roth-Händles,
that made a few
camels choke.
No carnal,
only during a
ritual where
the Spirit be,
otherwise it's
good-bye
marchangos,
dogs and wife.

Anyway, who would feed
el Gato Negro,
or play la concha
in New Year's snow?

pirámides—pyramid
carnal—brother; pal; buddy
marchangos—members of a Chicago-based Chicano arts organiza-
tion MARCH—el movimiento artistico chicano.
el Gato Negro—name Cortez gave his printing press; "Black Cat"
is one symbol of the IWW union.
la concha—the conch shell blown like a trumpet; a Nahuatl
musical instrument.

"Watch It Now, Watch It!"

Woolly Bully,
Sam the Sham and the Pharoahs

Cuento

Today I thought I'd call home
   so I got on the
      telephone
and said: "Operator please give me
   AZTLAN person to person"
She replied: "Sorry sir, still checking"
   after 2 minutes—
      She asked me to spell it—
So I did—
      A-Z-T-L-A-N
She thought I said ICELAND
at first but after the spelling she said
What?!!
      AZTLAN!
   She said is this some
   kind of a joke
      I said, "No, you
      know where it is"
   She said—"Sir I cannot
   take this call
But if you wish I'll
      let you talk to
my supervisor—"
      I said: "Fine
         Put 'em on
   I got time"—
Well her supervisor got on the line—
      And I told her what
I had said before
   All she could say was that
   was the first time she ever heard
   about it—I said, "You'll hear more
about it soon!"—and hung up—

**America needs "Operation Jobs,"
Lee Treviño found missing or
Pancho Villa—where are you now
that we need you?**

250 arrested on Tuesday,
100 seized on Monday,
The raid sites had been set on Sunday,
so thousands could be ousted
by the immigration forces.

Another page of raza humilation,
here in the windy city
of Chicano, Illinois.
It was mostly Mexicanos,
so no one will be missed
down in City Hall.

These sweeps only make good copy for a day,
but it has something to say
about making jobs available
the old American way.

Damn, what really gets me mad
is how Juan Valdez
was treated like a peon
by the press,
you know, our connoisseur of the coffee cup
was mistakenly grabbed,
I mean just picked up.
After all, you'd think they'd recognize him
from the commericals.

Now don't count on your restaurant meals
being made as fast as before,
'cause they just dragged
the entire kitchen crew
out the back door.

Out of the Closet Klan

Con verbal espinas
poking from his boca,
y cada palabra
smelling como pedos,
he went on
like a professional salesman
bent on scoring a commission.

Más que emociónes
spilt during our
evening of drinking,
y yo como un menso,
a polite one at that,
sitting potato-still,
listening to barato
bargain-basement assessments
on how to maintain
"our southern borders
from being overrun by
hungry brown foreigners"

"Si,' I agreed, 'They arrive
by the dozens, and in months
they're sendin' for their cousins—"
then poured another Corona.

For hours we sat,
a whole world away
from where the KKK

was patroling that day,
but los Chicanos
had already
changed the map.

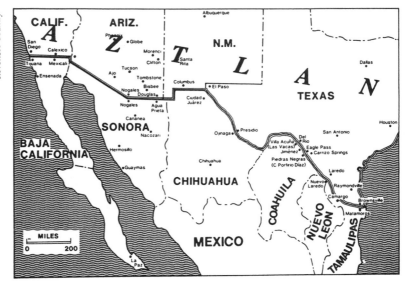

espinas—thorns, cactus spines
boca—mouth
y cada palabra—and each word
como pedos—like farts
más que emociónes—more than feelings (emotions)
menso—fool
barato—cheap

Veterano

Insect victories
fought over scum-cracked
concrete and colors
no one wants to see,
especially families in the park
as it gets dark, and the boys
make their runs for wine, reefer,
glue or some friendly doctor's pills.

Buzzed six to a car,
roaring past stoplights
so "Lil Juanito" can score
before there's no more
angel dust or 'cane
Tonight he got burned,
they might as well have sent
a drunk baboon on the deal.
"Pinche menso, why didn't you
check it?"
"Calláte tu hocico buey,
come caca
si no te gusta."
"Speak English cabron!"
"OK, con safos chicabacho."

It's swell-chest time and your pandilla
has got it bad, the magic markers are
almost empty and there's no more
white shoe shine.
The cross-town clubs, even the putos
from down the block, have painted

out your folk's marks.
So & so and so & so runs it,
there's hand signs and murder mouthing
and a fight for the crown,
when one of Beto's buddies lets you
know who runs it,
a fast blast from a stolen gun
then his slow life sentence.

Y tu en el mundo de mierda
piensas que eres muy cool
todos los chavos can't wait
to water down their lives for you,
pero you're always worried 'bout
who's watching your back
and if you'll hear the hammer go
click...

Didn't make it in school?
Trabajo ruins all your fun?
Change all that, get in with
the real gang-bangers' delight,
the original ruff-tuff stuff,
join up con ese locos in the Marines.
Those guys have got everything!
Camouflage and M-16's,
they've kicked ass from the sangron
"Halls of Moctezuma" to the
terrorist resorts of Tripoli.

So get mad, make revenge your cohort,
be "bad" and live with the ganga
of your pitiful choice,
even if your deepest friend—
your inner voice, tells you
to do otherwise.
Listen here, bato con la mota brain,
listen and you'll catch the
click—as its owner yells,
"Yanquí!"

cabrón—an insult (i.e. S.O.B.)
pinche menso—damn dummy
calláte tu hocico buey—shut your snout, ox!
come caca—eat shit
si no te gusta—if you don't like it
chicabacho—Chicano who acts and thinks Anglo
pandilla—gang
putos—male whores
chavos—young guys
bato con la mota—dude with the marijuana (brain)
Yanquí—Yankee

Comfortable & Politically Correct

What to wear, what to wear—
now let's see what's in the closet.
Bring down all the hangers,
pull off the scratchy labels,
Made or assembled in:
South Korea, Taiwan, Haiti,
Portugal, Phillippines, Peru,
Macao, Mexico, Singapore,
Brazil, Bangladesh, Ecuador—
boots from billion-dollar
debtor nations,
belts from military
dictatorships,
gloves (and baseballs) from
ungovernable tropics,
shirts from storehouses
of starvation wages,
coats from decomposing
Asian and African colonies,
pants from pauper
brown-lung ports,
socks from places where
it's rare to own a pair
much less shoes—
hell, I think I'll go
naked today.

¿Pork Que No?

The truck grunts like a pig,
the truck grunts like a pig,
and tar streets are roasting pits
for the driver carrying nitrates.
He has a whole gut of cancer
from eating bacon,
ham sandwiches,
and headcheese.
The truck grunts like a pig,
the truck grunts like a pig,
the driver is ordering
lechón for lunch,
but there's no compensation
for heartburn and
constipation.

Who expects more from
a grunting pig?
The bingo ladies and bowling leagues
want their B.L.T's,
so step on it.
The butchers' union wants a raise,
but the bottom's
dropped out of pork bellies.
The entire barrio is ready
for tamales, órale.

Jesus drove out demons
from a possessed man
into the fat of some swine,
who died like lemmings

in their plunge.
The Spanish were first to bring
pigs to the continent,
their pork caught on big
with the locals,
'cause some say it tastes cómo
human flesh.
Swine and wine go good together—
make for fine conversation,
'cause them pigs,
y'know,
is smart.

barrio—neighborhood (esp. with ref. to Chicanos/Latinos)
lechón—suckling pig
órale—let's have it; that's it; that's right!

El Cinco de Mayo
or L Sinko Day My O

Napoleon the third
was nappin' under
an amber vino haze,
as sips of cognac
curled in
his stomach,
cuando las noticias
of the battle en Puebla,
México...1862
(first week of May)
made its way to
his foreign orejas.
Napoleon's Imp-err-ial
plans to add more miles
under his size five crown
were put into question,
due to beaucoup mistakes.
The little king underestimated
what four thousand macheteros
with freedom on their minds
could do.
No, Napoleon de turd didn't get his
Empire through
resistance fire,
it was roasted in the
ancient bar-b-coatl of
Don Benito Juárez's
Zapotec coast.
Y de mala muerte,
old Max y Char
gave it all they royally had,

even to the wall.
At last they understood
Mexican red-green chile
will always be stronger
than the hardest French bread.
Now, the only good thing
those fools left behind
were some tunes to hot
Mariachi get-downs,
after being driven back to boats
heavy with their dead.

cuando las noticias—when the news
orejas—ears
beaucoup—many (French)
macheteros—peasants armed with machetes
coatl—serpent (Aztec)
Max y Char—Emperor Maximilliano and Empress Carlotta

Next Year in Jerusalem

I.
In keeping promises
to his constituents and
the memory of his great aunt,
he painted the sky teal.
After closing both Middle East
and Star Wars deals, he twirled
his pearl-handled pistol one last time,
a souvenir from
those "Death Valley Days"
before he was touched by a bunch
of hot, stiff-necked people,
a Nile-bled people,
a people who have been the
"Little Davids" of the desert,
even as adobes were splashed
with swastikas and oil,
in return for a nihilistic smile
rooted in Moses' law, the Koran, and Bible—
heavenly insurance that commitments would
be kept,
even if Rand McNally has to rename
a few countries on the map,
while the U.N. patrols some new
north and south
borders again.

II.
O' you Illinois boy,
Tampico-born and Dixon-raised,
  an Irishman's son
who never knew race relations went
sour in Chicago's 1919 gasoline heat.

Hey there, Hollywood Guv,
  were you really in love
with "The Gipper"?
You knew more about those
  Notre Dame games
than Mexican California's
chili-skinned history,
   Alta o Baja
it was never your
    Aztlan.

World traveler
without a map,
how about your greeting
mix-up in Bolivia,
thinking you were in Brazil—
at least you didn't eat
your tamales still in their
corn wrappers.

The stage lights
have grown dimmer,
beyond the TV and movies,
yet, your sun shone
in an executive position
as you slipped off for a nod..
it wasn't the finger
on the button I feared,
rather, your old forehead
pressing down.

The New Job

The voice on the end
of the line
is not mine.
Forget the name I gave
during our
greeting exchange,
just understand
on the part of this
9 to 5 actor there's
a real need to gain
a rave review,
measured in cash,
gathered after hundreds
of bills of lading.
So give me small satisfaction
as you answer,
but remember,
any comments you'll make
will be kept on record
like an F.B.I. tracer.
Up in the front office
they know the score,
if I can maintain
this steady pace,
I'm free to remain on
the books,
keep account of the wheels
that turn,
dial tones on the phone,
and rolls and rolls of
surnames, area codes—

If I crack my fingers
the snoopervisor shouts,
"Call some other Mr. & Mrs.,"
as we wrap up the night,
in our race for
circulation.

The Survivor: Anishinabe Man

They found a man
who lived in ten
doubled-lined garbage bags
filled with newspapers,
tossed by the downtown crowds,
making a nest for
"no one special,"
just a survivor,
a wastebarrel hunter,
who found the paper that
corporate America hauls
out daily, could cover
his people
across Turtle Island.

He had nine months of rent free
sleeping and eating,
real evidence "the city works,"
even in Christian
chowmein lines,
where "Jesus Saves" and
law 'n order tools
are sharpened just south
of the Loop.

This soul traveled as
illegal cargo of desire
under the iron horse hulk,
following raw rails until
crippled inside
our hawk-headed town.

He dreamed of Canada
where no exhausted
four wheels made
mad morning rushes
by the big lake.

With no passport,
no marketable wares,
unarmed in the hog's
heart, after winter-
iced eyelids and
dead-moon winds,
you Anishinabe, who's
name I did not catch.
You, pepper-haired warrior,
refused to die, to die
alongside
the once green slant
of the foul expressway,
where your sad
recycled abode
challenged elements and
strange arrows
of motorized millions,
who yesterday
offered small pox blankets
and other offensive coverage
in their reams
of ink-marked sheets.

Tracks in the Snow

Coyote used to be somebody—
but during the last war
he died and was reborn.

After he came back,
he found work
in one of the
terminals of
planned obsolescence...
where robots win
and workers are
permanently let go.

Over his uniform,
layers of old
jackets & jeans,
his jaundiced face an
ashtray for whiskers.
Two weak eyes find
relief beneath red goggles,
and the faded-leather
air-man's cap was what he wore
while over Cambodia.
He still won't reveal
what happened on those
missions, so many seasons
before he hobbled cold
in angry skin.

Today's flight will be in search
for that precious
winter commodity—warmth.

Especially since
plastic bags cover old socks
filling cardboard-lined shoes.

Coyote never liked shoes.
In Oklahoma,
he always wore boots.

After Wrestling Away Rain Forests

The sun shown its furnace face today,
drying tears across once moist lands
now buried by choking inches,
hard measures in this
meatmade town.

Industries singe air and seas
causing the earth's lungs—the trees
to collapse beneath
smokestack disease.

While Amazon's Kayapó
armed with arrows and spears
take aim against highway plans
that would flatten

--the primordial green
by forces profiled
in Fortune Magazine.
As skies disappear,
over Arctic circles,
Chicken Little's refrain
becomes a warning—

Tomorrow city sheep
will bathe before
commuting
to keep from fainting or
feeling ozone summer heat—

Say, there was a train crash today,
poison gas derailed,
workers caught inside
officials say, it may be too late
for exposed grey matter.

Property is Theft

I had just signed my lease
for another year,
making sure that property-
entrepreneur was square.

I began to read the fine print,
As my eyesight went to dreamland,
but at a premium.
Just then, from my TV screen...

"We interrupt this program to bring you
a special news bulletin. In conjunction
with national and loco po-lice
departments, this following message
is issued. Make no attempts to
change the channel, no protests
against the past, present, or future
will be tolerated. Acts contrary to
this order will be met with
full crisis measures."

Then a familiar voice came back on the air
to share this last remark,

"Dear viewers, I urge you all to
keep tuned to the same station,
remember, the law is the law.
We now return you to the program
in progress."

Suddenly, rumbles in the dark,
generators blow sparkshowers
from high voltage wires,
as transmitters rupture,
screen patterns skip in
rapid succession,
as the red-veiled moon
rose in the sky,
the world's largest antenna
rents my landlord's head.

In Less Than an Hour

All tortured with adrenalin,
beat out of breath,
slippery with sweat
running shoes packed
with mud and crap.

Only fifty minutes ago,
it was stalking urban terror,
shotguns on the register,
phantom of the gangway,
master of the bellowing command;
"Everybody freeze, this is a stick up!
Out with the wallets, watches, and rings,
shit, give me some booze and squares...
hell, I'll take everything.
First jerk that moves gets
a butter-coated bullet."

Out the door flying livewire,
drive, no looking back,
up a dead-end without a map,
blam, blam, blam,
you're the cops' target.

Stomach aches as they close in,
their flashlights cause your
pupils to shrink.

When they catch you after the crash,
they promise a beating before booking and
place you in handcuffs eager to tick-grip
your pounding wrists...

"He's capable of anything, tighten them so
he don't get away."
They could spin you into black water,
you begin to scream, almost like a spoiled
boy of ten, "Let me alone, I don't know
nuthin' 'bout no gun," plead and moan,
denial your bullshit defense,
"I don't know 'bout no gun, sir."
"Tell us where the gun is, tell us!"
"I didn't see no gun, I don't know."
The entire neighborhood wakes up
to a full moon and
this late-summer interrogation.

Brought out before a curious crowd,
they offer no support in your behalf,
instead they whistle and applaud
your shitty capture.

Hours later your cartilage rests,
but your soul is restless.
Had you used your silly west-side mind
a little better, thrown down
a taste more reason,
you wouldn't have looked so
dumb hugging the ground
alongside the Chicago
River squatting with
toxins like the toilet
in your cell.

Macrobiotics and Macropsychotics

Eden's scent is gone,
ten-thousand species
smother under civilization's
turbulent dark plume.

Needing food we have ruined
air, water, land,
through tar and asphalt, roaring steel
and gasoline bringing our
wheeled assault against
forest, prairies, dunes and deserts—

Ship routes have become superhighways,
spiraling paths of commodities
spread its virus
across once-habitable lands.

Good Doctor Control can't see
under his table of fat and security,
the growing shadows of hunger.
Glory hallelujah...Go team Go!
It's a home run...it's a touchdown,
a hole in one...what a knockout
punch...congratulations on your
promotion...Merry Christmas...
Happy Birthday...
Three, two, one, liftoff!...
"We will all feel the pinch,
there will NOT be
a cadillac and a 40,000 dollar home
for everyone,

simply
the planet will not bear it..."
Sister di Prima, you warned us.

Congested cities of tin and mud,
corkboard walls, jerrybuilt stalls,
markets filled with lean people
and the gleanings of monocrop labor.
One country grows coffee, then cocaine,
another bananas, then marijuana,
others like Nicaragua once sold blood.
But who knew assassination
flourished under objectives of the
Fortune 500?

The deluge has hit again,
this time it's in our veins.
The Ark of our health is
shipwrecked on shores of lies,
while the searching dove
died of pesticides.
Dietary dementia attacks immune
systems after traditional culture
crumbles under seduction of
contending East and West "uncles."
Here, the poor inherit another
generation of food stamps,
with continued hopes for pacification
between drinking, dope and lottery.
Colonial settlers become false friends,
offer native populations hot dogs
and pizza until it's time for bullets.

Coyote Rides the Bus

Bums rush through terminal station
when a final basalt straggler boards
wearing a gladrag some dead banker
donated to Goodwill in Little Rock,
Arkansas...
A former flasher special
letting big hands dissolve
inside deep pockets
where soap can't reach.

Like dull marbles he drops dusty
pennies and nickles
into the farebox.
There are no pearlies,
cat's-eyes, or steelies,
at the bottom of his
purple coin pouch.

Sitting sideways,
going forty,
the chumpchange mogul
stares out the window,
fingers his American
polyester lapel,
a suit made when Kennedy
was the shining knight
and this passenger had a
permanent address.

Leaving, he flops his palm open
asking for cab fare to pick up
his princess at the airport,
..."just back from Mardi Gras,"
not a bad line, so I fish for
some change, wondering if
this panhandler's potentate
won't be late.

As the bus door opened
he flips me a card with
three rows of hands making
mudra letters for the
deaf and dumb,
he grins and says,
"Don't worry about me,
I got lots of jobs, here's one."

Kilotons and Then Some

Bombs on hot and crowded Nagasaki
and Hiroshima.
Bombs on hated Hai-phong harbor and Hanoi.
Bombs on the Caribbean jewel Puerto Rico
for almost a century—
Bombs on the presidential building
of socialist Chile in '73.

Bombs off Mexico's Veracruz
shot by U.S. Marines in 1914.
Bombs over the once many starfish
of now-radiated Pacific isles.
Bombs over the Buddha's blood fields
in Cambodia.
Bombs over Christ's homeland of Palestine.

Bombs over the cactus and lizards
of the New Mexican desert.
Bombs under the Nevada oasis scattering
Las Vegas.
Bombs under the Utah Mormon paradise.
Bombs with no markings sold to
those with no future.

Bombs under the Mongolian Gobi desert.
Bombs under the Siberian rock ice.
Bombs on the heads of Afghanistan.
Bombs with Moslem moon and star
of Pakistan.

Bombs with designer shades from France.
Bombs with mantras and incense
reincarnates India.

Bombs from David's six-pointed star
into the oil rigs of Iraq.
Bombs with red stars over
rich rice fields of Asia.

Bombs with question marks
from South Africa's white elite.
Bombs with passages from the Koran
canned in Libya.
Bombs from the 14th century of lonely Iran.
Bombs from the illreputed saint
of North Korea Kim Il Sung.

Bombs with no consideration
from his cousins in South Korea.
Bombs of the underdeveloped nations
just laying around.
Bombs of the SuperPowers leaving them
dumb.
Bombs of the captive people getting louder,
Bombs of the captors making them captives.

Bombs with names such as "TRINITY, 666,
LITTLE BOY, BLISTER BUSTER, HEAVY
METAL, BAR-B-QUED."
Bombs blessed by drunk church sinners
with sweaty palms.
Bombs with no chance of ever learning a trade.
Bombs four days old on the discount table.

Bombs the kind you'll never see.
Bombs the ones you only have to listen to
once—
and you'll never hear again.

Propulsion

Those terrible obsidian hands
wrapped hardened steel,
a cobalt scope—
held tightly and aimed
at the innocent...
the guilty.

Bullets and arms readily
available for a small fee,
then a three or four week
processing period
as they check for past
convictions,
outstanding circumstances—
but soon you own
an arsenal,
legal and pernicious.

Once empty chambers,
now house the friction
and determined spit of
collision unleashed,
fully prepared to open
the wonder of fragile
skin—under a single shot.

Comanche Tells Coyote

for Camilo

**Out of Custer's entire 7th Calvary,
only a horse named Comanche
survived the battle of Little Big Horn.**

George Armstrong Custer
was called stubborn and troubled.
No matter, he was a leader, a range rider
with political ambitions.
Like others before him and many who
followed—he planned to go from
the battle field to Capitol Hill.

Custer rode west, heart convicted,
Manifest Destiny was good for the
glory of Centennial America.

His men of the 7th were seasoned in the
power behind rifles, pistols,
swords and bayonets.
The Civil War had not paralyzed them all.

Drawing closer to the gold river
near big Sioux skies,
the wind carried their sweaty scent
right toward the Sun dancers' camp.
There, Crazy Horse and other elders prayed
for the sacred pipe's protection,
before engaging
the white man's trespassing shadow.
Sitting Bull raised the great eagle banner
to a chorus of young warriors' Ho Ka Hay!

Soon clouds appeared after running feet
and pounding hooves stirred the
contested land with determined
enemies, which the 7th had come to
rout, yet, not one soldier escaped
the patriotic Lakota flint or
Cheyenne lead.

Proud hearts seeking no
dry reservation existence, no stale
government hand-outs, no broken
home of life-numbing whiskey,
were made to fight...

As they circled the last of the 7th,
both man and horse sang,
"Niathuau Ahakanith! Niathuau Ahakanith!
Oyate my people listen,
The whites are crazy, the whites are crazy,
Yellow Hair's whites are crazy!"

After Little Bighorn's echos
faded from earth that hot June Sunday,
all bluecoats were adrift,
Custer their compass, a broken boat
without oars, sunk beneath buffalo medicine,
while summer's gaunt weariness
turned a salty red across the
greasy grass.

Coyote Sun

para María Sabina
y Anne Waldman

Gathered on Oaxaca's
huarache-worn stones,
made smooth by the soles
of thousands of believers—
never resting on their petates,
but dancing the ceremonial mitote,
where inspired beats leaped from a drum
and the mushrooms of language sang
through a poet-priestess--
María Sabina, duality's sister.

We never chanted in a temaskal,
never bowed stripped down to a
fire in the sweatlodge as
steam rose from the
lightning bolt's navel
carrying bile and filth to
the bowels of the desert.

You read everything as you listened
to the Folkways record,
and like a bold sinvergüenza
you performed nuestra santa voz
indigena for los otros.

But, where were the hongos of vital skin,
episodes of enrapture with the
living word as prayers passed,
round the candlestar hut.

You missed the children's sweetgrass breath
that prepares the way for hot aguardiente
tobacco and food, humble gifts for the ritual
where old man armadillo watched
the Mazatecan sky, waiting for
his ever-young brother Coyote Sun
to come back up--
Coyote Sun who tricks the
night into chasing him.

María Sabina in a flower huipil
adorned with a headdress of
silver braids, aflame with the
medicinal and sacred herbs of Christ.

María Sabina, the one we
talked about so far from
your boulder,
María Sabina, who heard
the jasmine tongue of heaven,
raised her palms to the saints
then clapped and whistled
as the true fast-speaking one,
a psi-eyed woman,
the one
who knows Coyote Sun.

petate—straw mats
mitote—loud festivity
temaskal—sweat lodge (Nahuatl)
hongos—psychoactive mushrooms

Carlos Cumpián hails from San Antonio, Texaztlan. Presently, he's considered a Chicagoan due to his voting record. He coordinates MARCH/ Abrazo Press and "La Palabra" poetry and music series at Randolph Street Gallery and other venues. His poetry has been published by some of the country's spirited small press magazines, as well as in numerous anthologies, most recently, *After Aztlan* (David R. Godine, Publisher). His latest book is *Latino Rainbow: Poems about Latino Americans* (Grolier/Childrens Press, 1994).

To schedule a poetry reading by Carlos Cumpián or to receive a complete list of MARCH/Abrazo books, contact by fax (312)539-0013 or write:
MARCH, Inc.
P.O. Box 2890
Chicago, Illinois 60690